How To Stand Up For What You Believe:
A Teen-Ager's Action Guide

HOW
TO
STAND
UP
FOR
WHAT
YOU
BELIEVE:

ASSOCIATION PRESS

A Teen-Ager's
Action Guide

HERBERT J. DETWEILER
Former Chairman, Youth Research Committee
Union College Character Research Project

NEW YORK

How to Stand Up For What You Believe:
A Teen-Ager's Action Guide

Copyright © 1966 by
Ernest M. Ligon

Association Press   291 Broadway   New York   N.Y.   10007

Illustrations by Elizabeth Lee Johnson

Publisher's stock number: 1615

Library of Congress catalog card number: 66-20471

PRINTED IN THE UNITED STATES OF AMERICA

*This book is dedicated to
the more than 1,500 teen-
agers who made it possible,
and to the millions more
whose courage of conviction
is the hope of the world.*

Preface

The writing of this book is based on two broad assumptions. The first is that you are a teen-ager who is not content to be an insignificant little speck in that great big "blob" known as "The American Teen-Ager." The second is that you have intelligence and backbone and would like to at least *try* to do something to make yourself a more effective person in the teen-age world.

Have you ever wished that instead of just *telling* you that you should stand up for what you believe—which of course you already know—someone would give you some realistic suggestions as to *how* you can do it?

7

Do you ever find yourself thinking that maybe the kids are right who say that it just is not possible to maintain a strong set of moral standards "in this day and age"?

Have you ever been with a group of friends who decided to do something you felt very strongly was not a good thing to do, but you went along with the gang anyway because you did not know how to handle the situation and were afraid that if you said anything you might lose their friendship?

The material in this book was made possible because a group of outstanding high school young people, concerned about these same questions, decided to *do* something about them. Under the guidance of the Character Research Project of Union College in Schenectady, New York, they spent two years gathering data, sorting and analyzing, in search of answers to two crucial questions:

1. How can teen-agers stand up for what they believe, especially in the face of social pressure against those beliefs?

2. Are there certain skills teen-agers can learn that would enable them to do this in such a way that they would actually influence others to see their point of view, and to appreciate more fully the convictions upon which that viewpoint is based?

Before they were finished, these young researchers

had conducted more than 1,500 guided interviews with other teen-agers in all sections of the country, and had amassed over 6,000 written incidents of successful and unsuccessful attempts by teen-agers to stand up for what they believed. Working with the Character Research staff, eighty-eight of the best qualified young people then applied scientific tools of analysis to this mass of data at a Youth Research Congress. The book you have just opened is the result of this cooperative research effort. Thus, what you are reading is not just another book of adult advice to teen-agers. It is an action guide *from* teen-agers *to* teen-agers.

Note the words in the title of this volume: *"How* to Stand Up For What You Believe." The title assumes, of course, that you *do* have some beliefs! Therefore, you will not find in these pages a list of *what* those beliefs should be. The study that formed the basis of this book found that most young people are familiar with the "what"—they have at least a vague idea of right and wrong and can list some personal convictions. And in most cases they *want* to be more effective in standing up for their beliefs. If our evidence is correct, it is probably with the "how" that you need the most help. The purpose of this book is to show you the "how."

World events point increasingly to the fact that lasting peace and understanding among men cannot grow in a leadership vacuum. The most urgent present and future need is for leaders of imagination, courage, and goodwill. Above all, today's world requires men and women of strong conviction who have developed the skills necessary to influence others effectively as they seek to uphold those convictions. It is my earnest hope that, with the help provided in this book by your fellow teen-agers, you may become a part of the world's desperately needed moral and spiritual leadership.

There are two kinds of leaders. The obvious kind is the "drum major" variety, the guy or gal who is "up in front" of the group for all to see. But what about the key players in each section of the band or orchestra—the boy playing first trombone or the girl in the first violinist's chair? From the audience they look just like any of the other players, but they are the *leaders within* the group, persons to whom others look for guidance and inspiration. Every group or organization is like that. There are leaders who "stick out" and there are leaders within. You may be the type of boy or girl who would rather not be up front, and you may have, therefore, concluded that you are "just not a born leader."

Let it be said right now that the teen-agers who participated in this study were not, by and large, the kind who likes to say, "Hey, everybody, look at me! I'm the leader!" Rather, they were young men and women just like you, who in their own quiet way learned that the power of example is far greater than the power of speeches, and that a few well-chosen words often have greater influence than the loud oration.

Can you be this kind of leader? Can you really expect to have much influence for good? The teen-agers who produced the materials for this book answer with a resounding

YES, YOU CAN!

Peoria, Illinois   HERBERT J. DETWEILER

Acknowledgments

There are few completely one-man efforts in today's world, and this book is another testimony to that fact. The writer wishes at this time to acknowledge his debt to the multitude of people whose knowledge, skill, dedication, and just plain hard work made the writing a much simpler task.

Dr. Ernest M. Ligon, founder and guiding genius of the Character Research Project since its inception in 1935, was the dynamo behind the whole Youth Research Congress idea. Working closely with him on the research design for the Congress were research psychologists Dr. William A. Koppe and Dr. Leona J. Smith. Mr. Henry Giles, chairman of the youth department, and his assistant, Miss Suzanne Channell, organized and supervised much of the data gathering and post-Congress analysis. The typing, proofreading, and retyping of copy took many hours of skilled labor by many people.

But without the teen-agers themselves, who devoted more than 10,000 hours to this project, all the carefully constructed research designs and plans for analysis would have been for nothing. To them must go the deepest gratitude of all.

Contents

Page

1. The Power of Personal Convictions 19

What are *your* convictions? . . . Where do you
stand? . . . Significant or trivial? . . . What
characterizes a "successful conviction"? . . .
"Cost-difficulty" . . . Long-range dimension
. . . Broad moral principles . . . Growth and
flexibility

2. Are the Conditions in Your Favor? 59

The problems or situations . . . The "audience"
. . . Your home climate . . . Your reputation
. . . Cultivating a "service climate"

3. The Keys to Your Personal Power 77

Perceptual skills . . . Skills and characteristics
of personality . . . The skills of "image-building". . . General skills . . . Skills of evaluation

4. A Master Plan 121

Your philosophy of life . . . It's time to decide

CHAPTER ONE

The Power
of
Personal Convictions

The
Power
of Personal
Convictions

"As for me, give me liberty, or give me death!" These words of Patrick Henry helped to change the course of world history. They represent one of the most powerful "weapons" of the American Revolution.

What makes the declaration so powerful? Is it the words themselves? Only partly. There is an inner, compelling force one can almost feel coming through the words. It is this unseen power that gave these particular words such influence at the time they were spoken, and that has made them endure to inspire lovers of freedom throughout the world to this day.

What is this force? *It is the power that comes from having strong convictions and the courage to stand for those convictions, "no matter what."* This power of conviction in the "rightness" of their cause enabled a comparative handful of colonists to defy and defeat the armed might of eighteenth-century Britain. It is the same quality that makes us sit up and take notice when one person speaks while another, lacking such power, is virtually ignored. Look around you in your own community and school. Find the true leaders and you will find men and women, boys and girls, of strong conviction.

What Are Your Convictions?

Is that word "conviction" a familiar one to you? It is to most teen-agers; yet, if our research evidence is correct, few of them have ever applied the word to themselves in the sense of thinking through *their own* convictions. Almost everyone has *some* guiding principles or beliefs which determine the way he acts and thinks, whether he is conscious of them or not. Undoubtedly, there are some questions or issues about which *you* feel very strongly. Perhaps your feelings have been reflected in experiences similar to these two, reported by teen-agers in a national survey and, like all the true incidents reported in this book, quoted in the exact words of the interviewee:

During exams some of the kids in one of my classes were cheating and they asked me for some of the answers to the questions. I refused to help them because I feel cheating is wrong.

Several girls were talking about another girl. They said that she had a bad reputation, but she appeared to be a nice girl to me. I never believed in that "gossip" stuff, so I defended her. As a result, this girl is accepted. She is a wonderful person and we all treasure her friendship.

Do you remember the last time you were involved in a situation in which you found your own beliefs coming into conflict with the ideas or beliefs of another individual or, perhaps, with a group of individuals? Did you say or do something at the time simply because you felt very strongly that it was the "right" thing to do or say under the circumstances? That feeling of the "rightness" or "wrongness" of things comes from your *convictions*, and those convictions provide the power for your own ability to influence others—your "social influence skills."

Suppose Patrick Henry had said, "Well, I'm not sure how I feel about this business of taxation and the King's demands. Let me think about it for a while and I'll let you know." These are hardly words to light the flames of freedom. But the Virginian had the power of conviction behind him, and when he spoke, the effect was felt clear around the world!

Where Do You Stand?

When you are not sure where you stand on a question or in a given situation, the chances are that either you will remain silent and "go along with the crowd," or you will make a weak protest that accomplishes nothing.

How do we know this? Because that was the most important single finding of the study upon which this book is based. IN ORDER TO INFLUENCE ANYONE WHEN YOU ARE FACED WITH SOCIAL PRESSURE TO ACT AGAINST YOUR CONVICTIONS, YOU MUST FIRST HAVE SOME CONVICTIONS FOR WHICH TO STAND! No convictions—no power!

This statement may seem so obvious that it need not be said, but it is surprising how few persons, adults as well as young people, ever sit down to ask themselves the question, "What do I believe in?" which is another way of saying, "What are my convictions?"

What, then, is a conviction, and how does a conviction differ from an ordinary opinion? The dictionary defines a conviction as "a strong persuasion or belief"; but an opinion is simply "what one thinks or believes about something." In the following statement it is evident that the *strength* of the belief makes the difference. This is the definition of a conviction used by the teen-age researchers in this study: "*A conviction is a principle of action concerning the righteousness of which I am convinced—so convinced that I am willing to live by it.*"

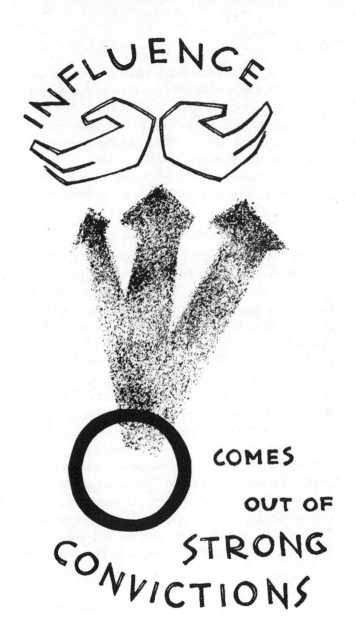

INFLUENCE

COMES OUT OF STRONG CONVICTIONS

Action!

Now, what about you? Have you ever tried to put into words how you feel about life? If someone were to ask you point-blank, "Is there anything you believe in so strongly that you are willing to risk your life for it?" what would you reply? What are the general principles or beliefs by which you have tried to "steer" your life up to now? Have any of them changed in the past few years? How will you know when they should be changed or modified in the future?

KEEP A "PHILOSOPHY OF LIFE" NOTEBOOK

In order to make the most of your investment of time in reading this book, you need to be thinking about your answers to these and other related questions. One of the best ways other teen-agers have found to organize their thoughts and keep them handy for later reference is to start what we will call a "Philosophy of Life" notebook. This will be a continuing record of your developing convictions and philosophy of life. If you do not happen to have a notebook on hand at the moment that can serve this purpose, a few sheets of plain paper will get you started. Then you can transfer the material to your notebook later.

Since each person is unique, no two people will organize their notebooks in exactly the same way. You may wish to divide yours into various broad areas of conviction, such as "religious," "social," "vocational." Or, perhaps, a better division for you would be the four general areas of life: physical, mental, spiritual, and social. Of course, it is entirely possible that you will not want to set up any specific divisions as such, but will prefer to keep your notebook as a sort of diary of your developing thought. The important thing is that you should have some special place in which to record your deepest thoughts and convictions. This will help provide the power by which you can become a stronger, more effective person; and you will also find that watching your own mind at work as it struggles with some of the basic questions of life is thoroughly fascinating.

SPECIAL NOTE: Remember that you are setting up a book to which you will be returning again and again over the years. So as you make your initial entries, you may want to write on only the right-hand page of each two facing pages, leaving the left-hand page blank. Then, as you rethink and revise that particular conviction or idea later on, you can enter the changes on the adjacent page. In this way, you will be able to follow more easily your expanding ideas. Another practical suggestion is to number each page. Then if you run out of room on one page, you can insert a notation, "continued on page—." This, too, will help you to keep track of a particular train of thought.

MAKE A LIST

Would you like to get some idea of how much power you have right now to back up the social influence skills you will learn about shortly? Take a sheet of

MAKE A LIST

paper and list the ideas or beliefs about which you feel the strongest. Do not worry for the moment as to whether or not a particular idea is really a conviction or just an opinion. The important thing is to get some ideas with which to begin. As we go along you will begin to see the distinction a little more clearly. If you have difficulty finding the words to start your list, perhaps it will help to consider some of the basic documents in our national heritage, such as the Declaration of Independence, the Constitution, or the Bill of Rights. Are there some ideas here that you can put into your own words? What does your religious faith have to say about some of the basic ideas of life? All these things should help give you a starting place. When you have completed this initial list, keep it handy, for you will be using it immediately.

Significant or Trivial?

Now take another look at the convictions you have just written. Are they of equal importance, or do some seem rather trivial when compared with others? What makes the difference? Perhaps that history-making gentleman of strong conviction can provide an illustration.

Suppose Patrick Henry had expressed the feeling that his home colony of Virginia was more beautiful than the colony of Pennsylvania. This is an *opinion*, and, likely, one he would not have gone to very great

27

lengths to defend. But when he felt that men should not have to live under oppressive rules and regulations set by an absentee government in which they had no voice, it was quite a different matter. This is such a strong *conviction* that he was willing to stand up and declare to all the world his uncompromising stand that liberty is worth dying for.

It becomes evident, then, that *some convictions are worth more than others.* Some are little more than personal opinions, while others concern principles of such basic importance that one is willing to make great sacrifices to uphold them.

One of the steps used in the analysis of the research data upon which this book is based was to list all the convictions represented by the incidents of attempted social influence the teen-agers reported and then to rank them in terms of their significance to society. Two of the ninety-five convictions are listed below; one of them was ranked very high in significance and the other much lower.

1. Class meetings and elections should use democratic methods.

2. Everyone should be able to have his own beliefs.

Which of these two convictions do you feel is more significant to society? If you chose the second one you agree with the researchers. Every conviction can be ranked in a similar way, using some criterion.

Action!

You may find it interesting to take your own list of convictions and rank them. Perhaps you will want to use the same criterion that was used in this research: How significant is this conviction to our society? Or you may prefer to develop your own criterion. Whatever you use as a "measuring stick," place a number "1" beside the conviction on your list that you think is the most important to your criterion, a "2" beside the next most important, and so on down to the conviction you feel is the least important. When you have completed this process, take another look at the convictions you put in the lower portion of the ranking. Are some of them really only opinions? If so, you may want to drop them from your list. Also, as you add to the list from time to time, you might ask yourself: Where does this new conviction fit in the ranking of importance?

IN A NUTSHELL

The most important thing we have found so far is that the skills of social influence must have the power of conviction behind them or they will not work. And these convictions must be important enough to earn the attention and respect of the people one is trying to influence.

What Characterizes
a "Successful Conviction"?

Almost no one is sucessful every time he attempts to stand up for what he believes. This was true of the teen-agers whose experiences provided the basis for this research and, no doubt, it has been true of you. But did you ever try to figure out *why* you were successful in some cases and not so successful in others?

Some of the most surprising findings from the research concerned the factors that *did not* prove important. Never once in all the thousands of cases that were examined did any of the following characteristics play a *decisive* role in determining whether a teen-ager was successful in standing up for what he believed:

> Physical attractiveness
> Personal charm
> High IQ
> High socioeconomic status
> Race
> Age

Of crucial importance, apparently, was *the nature of the convictions themselves*. We have already seen that convictions vary considerably in their importance to society. There are other qualities or characteristics by which a conviction may be described. In this section we are going to list and illustrate the characteristics that were found to be consistently true of those convic-

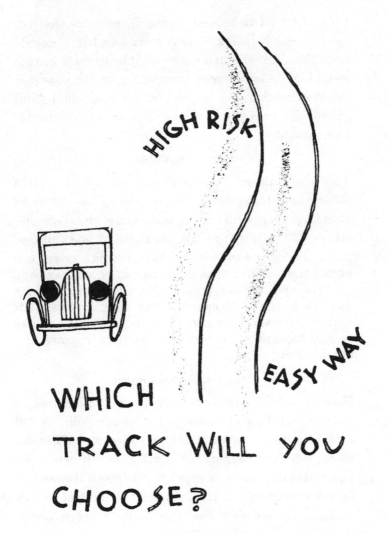

HIGH RISK

EASY WAY

WHICH TRACK WILL YOU CHOOSE?

tions that led to success in social influence. As they are discussed, take a look at your own list of convictions. You can obtain a fairly reliable estimate of your own chances for success in standing up for your convictions by checking to see how many of these "successful characteristics" you can find in each conviction on your list.

"COST-DIFFICULTY"

This characteristic, which stands out above all the others, asks the question, "How much could I lose by standing up for this conviction under these circumstances?" Contrary to what you might at first suppose, the evidence indicates very strongly that WHEN YOU STAND FOR A CONVICTION THAT INVOLVES A GREAT DEAL OF RISK AND IS VERY DIFFICULT TO UPHOLD, YOU ARE FAR MORE LIKELY TO REALLY INFLUENCE OTHERS THAN WHEN YOU HAVE VERY LITTLE TO LOSE OR WHEN THERE IS PRACTICALLY NO OPPOSITION TO YOUR BELIEFS AND CONVICTIONS.

Some Examples From History

Because this finding is of such crucial importance to the successful use of your social influence skills, we will look at it from several different viewpoints. First, let us consider once again that gentleman with whom we began this discussion of convictions. One of the reasons for his influential position in history is the fact that in standing up for his convictions he deliberately risked everything, even life itself.

Patrick Henry was a very successful lawyer in Virginia. Many of his friends and business associates, as well as a sizable segment of the populace (the "Tories," as they later came to be known), held allegiance to King George III. Henry had already been accused of treason by fellow members of the Virginia House of Burgesses during the debate over the Stamp Act of 1765, and no one had to tell him the penalty for treason to the throne! Thus, ten years later, when he stood up in the second revolutionary convention in his home colony and made his impassioned plea for liberty, he knew very well that it could put his neck in a hangman's noose. He could have taken the "safe" moderate position, as did many of the delegates, and no one would have thought any less of him. After all, a man had to think of his family and his future, especially a man with a wife and six children! But for Patrick Henry, conviction had to take precedence over *everything* else, including his own life. Because he stood for his convictions at great personal risk, "Give me liberty, or give me death!" became a rallying cry for all lovers of freedom, and Patrick Henry himself lives in history as a personification of courageous patriotism who has influenced unnumbered people far beyond his own place and time.

In his book, *Profiles in Courage,** President John F.

---

*New York: Harper and Row, 1961.

Kennedy gave us inspiring stories of men of American history, famous and obscure alike, who had to make similar decisions, this time at the risk of their political lives. One of the famous names is that of the great orator and senator, Daniel Webster, whose decision to support the Clay Compromise of 1850 quite possibly saved the United States as a nation by postponing the Civil War for ten years. But in standing for his conviction that the Union must be preserved at all costs, Webster knowingly committed political suicide. He was subjected to the most vicious public and private criticism. Not a single one of his political friends in New England had the courage to stand by him. He was abused in the press and, in a torrent of private correspondence, accused of being a traitor to the abolitionists' cause which he had wholeheartedly supported before 1850. Perhaps the highest cost of his courageous stand was the fact that it dealt a death blow to his most cherished ambition—the Presidential nomination from his party—a dream for which he had worked more than twenty years. Failing to achieve this high honor at the Whig convention in 1852, Daniel Webster died a discouraged but resolute man before the year was out.

Of the relatively unknown and obscure men who forsook the safety of their political careers for the sake of principle and conviction, none shines brighter in the light of history than Edmund G. Ross. A freshman senator from the frontier state of Kansas, Ross faced a particularly bright future as a public figure in the spring of 1868. In the words of the late President Kennedy, he was "... a man with an excellent command of words, an excellent background for politics, and an excellent future in the Senate." Yet, he turned his back on this potentially brilliant career and saw it dashed forever by the utterance of just two words. But by voting "not guilty" at the impeachment trial of President Andrew Johnson, Edmund Ross provided more than just the vote that saved a President. His act, along with that of six other courageous senators, saved the constitutional system of "checks and balances" from the threat of radicalism that followed the Civil War.

Ross had been warned repeatedly that to vote for acquittal would be to throw away his entire career. Moreover, he intensely disliked Andrew Johnson, who was a member of the opposition party, and he disagreed with the President's policies. Why, then, did he deliberately vote against the "popular" sentiment of the people and in defiance of the merciless pressure brought to bear upon him by his colleagues?

Perhaps an incident from the time will help to answer that question. On the night before the crucial vote was to be taken in the impeachment trial, Senator Ross received the following telegram: "Kansas has heard the evidence and demands the conviction of the

President. Signed, D. R. Anthony and 1,000 others."
To this Ross replied: "To D. R. Anthony and 1,000
others: I do not recognize your right to demand that
I vote either for or against conviction. I have taken an
oath to do impartial justice according to the Constitution and laws, and trust that I shall have the courage
to vote according to the dictates of my judgment and
for the highest good of the country." For his act of
courage Edmund Ross was repudiated by his party
and subjected to frightful humiliation in the press
and from individuals and groups around the country.
He was never again elected to public office, and when
he and his family returned to Kansas in 1871 at the
end of his first and only term, they "suffered social
ostracism, physical attack, and near poverty." It was
not until many years later, just before his death, that
a wiser nation tendered its belated gratitude to a man
who had shown extraordinary courage of conviction
under the most extreme conditions of difficulty.

Lest you jump to the hasty conclusion that only
men possess the power of conviction, let us briefly consider two examples from the distaff side. Few stories
in history stand out more forcefully than that of Joan
of Arc, a sixteen-year-old peasant girl, humble and
illiterate, who became convinced that God had called
her to perform a special mission. All of us know how
she overcame numerous obstacles to see the Dauphin
crowned, and then inspired the forces of her beloved

king to drive the English out of France. Captured and betrayed, at nineteen she faced a fiery death with faith and courage.

Susan B. Anthony also had a goal of liberation. She wanted to free the American woman from the "double standard" imposed by men and, especially, to gain for women the right to vote in a "free" country. Susan grew up in a strict Quaker home where women and children were taught to "know their place." Quaker belief was so rigid at the time that her father was expelled from membership because he allowed his home to be used as a place for giving dancing lessons! (He was opposed to dancing, but even more opposed to drinking. Since the only other place for the dancing class was in the hotel, where the young men and women might be tempted by strong drink, he decided that dancing was the lesser of the two evils and consented to the use of his home for the lessons.)

Early in her teens Susan decided that if women were ever going to achieve their full status on an equal basis with men, someone was going to have to sacrifice marriage and family in order to devote herself to a crusade for women's rights. She eventually decided that she herself would have to be the "someone." She was made a laughing stock, held up to ridicule and scorn, but the strength of her conviction would not let her quit. Even when she was arrested, tried, and convicted in New York State for the "crime" of voting, she did not lose her determination. Ultimately, her lifetime battle resulted in the Nineteenth Amendment to the Constitution, adopted in 1920, which guarantees the right of suffrage to all, regardless of sex.

What About You?

"This is all very well," you may be thinking, "but I'm not a Patrick Henry, an Edmund Ross, or a Susan B. Anthony. I don't have to risk my neck, and I don't have a political career. I am just a teen-ager trying to live as best I can in my own world of home, school, and community. How does 'cost-difficulty' apply to me?"

To illustrate how it applies, here are two examples from the Youth Survey data. The first is an experience related by a boy from the southwestern part of the country:

> I was working at a scout camp in the South. The last week was the session for Negroes. The white staff had quite a few qualms about the week. As the week progressed, I found that the Negro boys were no different than their white predecessors. My observations to this effect caused quite a bit of discussion.
>
> As a result, I lost no friends and, in fact, gained respect for standing up for what I believed right. Few agreed with me, but some progress was made. Ben Franklin was right when he said, "a turtle only makes progress when he sticks his neck out."

As an afterthought, he adds:

I was not on a crusade for justice, but just stated what I believed right in a frank manner. No one ever loses respect for honesty.

The second incident was written by a girl:

When my sister's teacher asked the class to write a 500-word paper on sororities, she was all for it. She came home and wrote an excellent paper on why *not* to join a sorority, knowing all the time that the other kids in the class were writing on the goodness of sororities. Classtime came and she read her paper out loud!

Some of the kids agreed with her points, and yet a lot of others criticized her up and down.

Both of these young people were taking a large risk in standing for their convictions. To be sure, they were not in much danger of losing their lives. Rather, the risk they ran is one that is much more real for teen-agers—*the risk of social disapproval and ostracism from "the group."* Time after time, when those interviewed in the National Survey were asked to list the *worst* thing that might have happened to them had they taken a given course of action, the answer came back in words similar to this girl's: "They could have called me 'chicken' and I would lose their friendship."

This is a very understandable concern. All of us like to be well thought of by our friends and associates. Teen-agers, particularly, feel the need to be liked and admired. One of the most coveted awards in many schools is to be voted "the most popular" boy or girl. Yet, the research evidence reminds us that "popularity" and long-lasting respect and admiration do not necessarily go together. There is a fickle quality about much popularity. If a poll is taken during the football season, the star halfback and the prettiest cheerleader or majorette usually take the popularity prizes. A few months later they are just two of many hundreds of students, and more recent "heroes" have taken their places on top of the popularity pedestal.

On the other hand, the kind of respect that the young man gained from the other camp staff members or that the girl earned by being willing to speak out when she knew that most members of the class were opposed to her views, will still be remembered by their associates long after any surface kind of "popularity" has evaporated.

CAUTION! It is important that you understand clearly at this point just what the research evidence is saying. It *does not* say that standing up for your convictions is an "open sesame" to popularity. On the contrary, you may often find yourself standing virtually alone on the unpopular side of an issue, like the girl in the following incident:

In a class discussion concerning civil rights with a group of strong "southern anti-Negro" students, I spoke out for the Negro's right to equal education opportunity. As a result, I lost all social acceptability with this group.

Nor does the evidence indicate that *everyone* respects courage of convictions If you look at life realistically, you know that there always seem to be some individuals who tease and ridicule those who are trying to stand for what they feel is right. Psychologists tell us this is often a mask to cover up one's own feelings of inadequacy or embarrassment, but this fact does not make the ridicule any easier to take.

The findings of this research *do* say that if you would rather have a sincere kind of respect from the thinking members of the group whose opinions you value the most, and if you aspire to be a genuine influence in helping them to see the value of your convictions, then the more difficult it is to stand for those convictions in a given situation and the greater risk you run in doing so, the greater will be your chances for success.

There is much "common-sense" reasoning behind this principle. Every individual, whether he is aware of it or not, has what is called a "value system," a kind of mental yardstick by which he determines what is important, and how important it is to him. A set of convictions is an important part of this "system." Because society is composed of groups of individuals, we can say that the society itself tends to have certain general values, based upon the measurement scale that seems to be the most commonly held by its members.

In our own society, we tend to judge the value of an item by its cost, usually in terms of money. A deluxe sports car carries a great deal more "status" and prestige than a bicycle, because it is much more expensive. Another bit of evidence that indicates something about our system of values is the fact that if we want to impress a young man with the importance of a college education, we do not get a very strong response by talking about its broadening his horizons or making him a better citizen. Instead, we tell him that a college degree could increase his lifetime earnings by as much as a quarter of a million dollars!

But there are other methods of "payment" besides money. If you set as your goal the attainment of the first chair in a certain section of the school band or orchestra, or a first-string position on the varsity team, you know that this achievement must be paid for by many hours of hard practice and self-discipline. It follows, then, that the more one is willing to pay for something, either in money, time, hard work, social position, or some other valuable consideration, the more we tend to think, "That surely must be important to him if he is willing to put so much into it."

This is why others are impressed when you are willing to risk losing something of as great value to teenagers as status in the group or friendships, in order to maintain the self-respect that comes in knowing that you have been true to your convictions and stood for what you felt was right, even in the face of great pressure to do otherwise. People tend to think, "This must be awfully important to him if he's willing to risk losing his friends for it. Maybe I should think twice about it myself." Through this process, you become a greater influence in the group.

Action!

This means, of course, that you are going to have to decide just how much each of your convictions is worth—what you will risk for them. At this point, you may want to take another look at your list. Read the conviction you have ranked at the top in terms of importance. What is it worth to you? Would you be willing to pay with your life in order to uphold it? Is it worth your being left standing all alone on the unpopular side of an issue, perhaps laughed at and ridiculed? The evidence indicates that you need to make these decisions *now*, because you probably will not have time to debate them in your mind when the occasions arise that will force you to take a stand.

Convictions with a long-range dimension are more effective than those with a short-range point of view. This is another very important principle, and often means the difference between success and failure in standing up for your beliefs. What do we mean by "long-range dimension?" Essentially, this means thinking beyond your immediate desires, and considering the long-range effect of your actions. Do you know teen-agers whose major guiding principle in life seems to be "I believe I should be allowed to do whatever I want to do whenever I want to do it"? Actually, this philosophy belongs to the baby stage of development. We expect babies to exhibit an "I want what I want when I want it" attitude. They know nothing else. But by the time a person has grown to teen-age, he should be able to take a little longer range look at life, as shown by the girl who related the following incident:

> This took place in a small town in Italy, near an Army base. As a group of (American) boys and girls were walking home from a house party, some of the boys wanted to try their luck at knocking out streetlights. I was set against it from the time they first stated what they intended to do. I told them that they would be destroying not only property which didn't belong to them, but also would be ruining the relations between the Americans and the Italians. And the main reason we were overseas was to help strengthen our relation-

44

LONG RANGE

SHORT RANGE

POINT OF VIEW

DIMENSION

ship, not destroy it. They listened to me, and we continued walking down the street until we reached our homes.

As a result, I believe that a small dot or dent was made in helping to better foreign relations. The kids all respected me more and in the future I was looked up to and often consulted on problems which came up.

In this case the girl was able to see immediate benefit from her stand, in the form of changed behavior. In the following incident a boy had the same long-range principle in mind, but the results are not quite so obvious:

A man who lives a few houses down the street from me asked me to rake his lawn and he would pay me five dollars. I told him that I would rake it, but only for three dollars because it wasn't worth five dollars.

It changed this man's idea that teen-agers had to be paid outrageous sums of money to do work. In my estimation he has a higher regard for teen-agers now.

Would you have taken the five dollars and said nothing except, perhaps, "Thank you?" Many teen-agers would. But think how this one unselfish act may have affected not only the man involved in this situation, but other people to whom he might relate the incident. It may well have been the best two-dollar investment this boy will ever make! Such is the additional power to be gained by looking beyond the present.

Interestingly enough, this ability to take the long view and consider the long-range effects of one's immediate wants and actions is one of the signs of a mature and well-adjusted individual, according to leading psychologists. Contrast the feeling of maturity that came through as you read those last two incidents with the impression you get about the teen-ager involved in the following one:

> I stood up for something that I believed to be right when my sister, my neighbor, and I were watching television and a cartoon show came on. For some reason I despise cartoon shows, so I changed the channel. My sister did not like to watch the other channel, so my sister got slapped by me. This I know was wrong but, as I said, I despise cartoon shows.

No doubt this action was effective in achieving the desired immediate goal. But what do you suppose its effect was upon the long-range relationship between sisters? The chances are that if the girl who related this incident had stopped to consider her action, she would have decided that it was not worth jeopardizing the years she had to live with her sister for the sake of one short cartoon show.

In summary, then, it can be stated that if your convictions seem primarily aimed at the immediate satisfaction of selfish goals, what little success you have will tend to be short-lived. On the other hand, if you will cultivate the habit of taking the long look, and will reflect this habit in your convictions, you are much more likely to be of lasting influence in your everyday relationships.

Convictions based on broad moral principles carry more influence than those which are simply miscellaneous "rights and wrongs."

When a building is being constructed, the builder does not start right in and put up one wall here, another over there, and still a third somewhere else. He first constructs a broad foundation upon which each of the individual walls and supports can securely rest. Developing a set of meaningful and effective convictions involves a similar process. First must come the broad moral principles which form your basic philosophy of life. Then, building upon this foundation, you can begin to develop specific convictions.

Very often in the National Survey data, teen-agers would express convictions in terms similar to these: "I don't think it's right to smoke," or "I don't think you should drink," or "It's wrong to park." These people were likely to be less successful in their efforts to influence others than those whose convictions were based upon broader principles, such as "I try to avoid *any* habits which might injure my health," or "Boys

48

should always treat girls with respect and responsibility."

We received many reports relating to race relations. Statements like "You shouldn't be prejudiced," or "It's wrong to hate Negroes," were usually the tip-off to an unsuccessful incident. The girl in the following situation, however, exhibited the kind of broad philosophy of race relations that is much more successful in carrying influence in this admittedly difficult area.

> Several of my friends are Negroes. Today one of the guys (I met him when our youth groups met together) came out of an aisle in the theater where we had just had a history movie. He said something to me and we walked up the steps together, talking. I know I risk losing respect from some of my very good friends who are prejudiced, but I think I'm not worrying about small things like such a selfish fear. I *briefly* explain if any of my friends says something to me concerning this. Trying to set an example which may help them lessen their prejudices is another motivation which gives me strength to live up to my ideals, keep them always in sight.

This girl's quiet example speaks "louder" than any lecture or speech she might have given her friends about the evils of prejudice and, undoubtedly, carries considerably more influence.

Once again it is important to interpret the data correctly. It should not be implied that having a set of "do's and don'ts" or feeling that certain things are "right" or "wrong" is undesirable. This is *not* what the findings indicate. Perhaps we can best illustrate the way in which this characteristic makes a difference by calling once again upon an actual incident. A girl reported:

> My group of friends were planning a drinking party and I felt they were wrong. I got quite angry and told them off. I told them that drinking was a cheap thrill and I felt they should have more respect for themselves than to go around drinking at fifteen and sixteen just to be big. They called me a prude and stuck up. I told them as long as they went through with it I wanted no part of them.

Quite obviously, this is not the way to "win friends and influence people." Why was this girl not successful in standing for her convictions? One reason, of course, is the manner in which she went about it, making them feel like little children being scolded by their mother. We will deal with more effective social influence skills in this area a little later. But perhaps a more significant and basic reason is that she attacked a specific "wrong," rather than putting it into a larger perspective and seeing it in relation to a broader moral principle. Suppose she had said something like this in a calm voice and without a trace of "bossiness": "I think the party idea is great, but I can't see the fun of waking up the next morning feeling guilty and nursing a 'big head.' Why don't we have Coke and pizza? I'll make one of the pizzas. Mary, how about making the other one?"

If you had been in this group or a similar one, how would you have reacted to this second, more broadly-based approach? It would have been difficult to call her a "prude" or "stuck-up" in this case, wouldn't it?

When you are dealing with controversial subjects in particular, a broader-based stand will lead to much greater success and more enduring influence.

GROWTH AND FLEXIBILITY

Teen-agers whose convictions are growing and expanding are more influential than those who are rigid in their ideas. Young people who approach situations with a spirit of openness to new ideas are much more successful in influencing others than those whose approach gives the feeling, "I have all the answers. My mind is made up, so don't try to show me anything different!" Following is an example of a boy who, though he had a definite opinion in this fairly common situation was, nevertheless, flexible enough to see another point of view and to profit from it.

A teacher gave me a B-plus on my report card when I thought I deserved an A. When I questioned him on this he said I deserved an A but he didn't "want me to feel too good." Also, he said he would rather have me go up than down. I said OK, and strove to do an even better job.

51

GROWING IN MATURITY

Whether or not the teacher in this situation was justified in his action is not our concern here. The point is that the boy was able to use the incident as a stepping-stone instead of a stumbling block because he remained open to a different way of thinking.

It has been said that "growth is the only evidence of life." We are surrounded by examples of this principle in the world of nature. A plant that ceases all growth activity soon dies. Animals, including the human variety, are always in the process of growing (if not in stature, at least in such areas as the growth of hair and nails and the regeneration of tissue). When such growth stops, the creature is dead.

Do you know people, young or old, who are spiritually or intellectually "dead" by this definition—people whose ideas have stopped growing? Often, they express their feelings in this way: "There is no use trying to convince me; this is what I have believed since I was a child, and I just *know* it's right!"

This finding has very important implications for you as you seek to develop a meaningful set of convictions. How does one become convinced about something? If a friend walks up to you in the hall at school and discloses some surprising news, your first reaction is likely to be "How do you know?" In other words, you want some *evidence*. If your friend can produce evidence which you accept as valid, you are more likely to accept his statements as being true. You have become *convinced* by the *evidence*.

It is vitally important to remember, however, that evidence is very seldom absolutely final. There is always the possibility that new evidence will develop which will cause you to change your ideas. Every scientist in every research laboratory is literally betting his life that this is the case. To be sure, some people use this fact of change as an excuse for not taking the time to think through their beliefs. They say, "Everything is relative. There are no final truths. So why should I try to set up a code of beliefs or convictions?" The answer, of course, is that without some sort of convictions to serve as guidelines, you are like a ship without a rudder, drifting first this way and then that, driven by whatever happen to be the prevailing winds and currents of social pressure and so-called "public opinion."

What you must do, then, is to take a cue from the scientist, and set up a "hypothesis." It should go something like this: "These are the best convictions I can discover on the basis of the present evidence, and I am willing to live by them, even in the face of pressure to do otherwise. At the same time, I will remain open to new evidence, since I know that one measure of my growth toward maturity is the increasing depth and breadth of my convictions."

Action!

Here is a long-term project which you can carry out in order to determine whether or not you are growing and developing in your ideas and beliefs. As these next weeks and months go by, set a regular time, such as the first Sunday of every month, for "Idea Inventory." During this time, read over your convictions and ideas. Have you changed your mind at all about any of them? Have you thought of a better way to express your current thinking? What new thoughts have come to you as a result of the experiences you have had, the books you have read, or the conversations you have shared during the past days or weeks? Jot these down opposite the appropriate item in the notebook, or start new pages.

Five years from now, as you look back over this record of your mind at work, you should find almost nothing with which you still agree *completely*. If none of your major concepts show signs of growth and development over this five-year period, perhaps you have stagnated and are in danger of spiritual or intellectual "death." On the other hand, if you are conscientiously searching for new truth and are open and responsive to new ways of looking at life and life's problems, your chances of influencing others effectively will be greatly enhanced.

One of the major factors in determining whether or not teen-agers are successful in standing for their convictions has to do with the nature of the convictions themselves. The four characteristics below were found to be consistently true of those convictions which led to successful attempts to influence others.

1. The more difficult the conviction is to stand for, and the greater the risk involved in doing so, the greater is the chance of success.

2. Convictions which reflect a concern for the long-range effect of one's actions lead to more effective influence than those which seem only concerned with immediate results.

3. Convictions based upon broad moral principles carry more influence than those that are simply miscellaneous "rights and wrongs."

4. Teen-agers whose convictions are growing and expanding are more influential than those who are rigid in their ideas.

Measure your own convictions by these characteristics, and you will obtain a good estimate of the amount of power you will have behind your skills of social influence.

CHAPTER TWO

Are the Conditions in Your Favor?

Are the
Conditions
in
Your Favor?

If you were an astronaut preparing to be rocketed beyond the friendly cover of the earth's atmosphere, you would be very careful to make certain that all the conditions were just right to assure the maximum chance of success for your mission. Is the life-support system working properly? Can you depend on your guidance and control systems? What about the condition of the booster rocket itself?

Similarly, a high school athlete whose goal is to set

a new record in a track and field event knows that his chances for success are directly related to the conditions existing at the time he makes his assault on the record book. What is the condition of the track? What about wind velocity and direction? Is he "just right" both physically and mentally? Against whom will he be running or jumping, and how do they usually perform? Will he need to pace himself and, if so, has a plan been worked out and practiced?

Details? Certainly. But just as in the worlds of space and athletics the details make the difference, so in the area of social influence there are certain details or conditions that can make the difference between influencing others effectively and wasting your power in frustration and embarrassment. To be sure, you cannot always predict or control all these conditions, but many of them you *can* do something about. A farmer does what he can to make his soil the most productive possible. At the same time, he makes it his business to know which of many different crops grow best under varying conditions. Then when he encounters certain soil or other conditions on his land, he knows just the right seed to plant to take the fullest advantage of the growth possibilities afforded by those particular conditions. Similarly, by knowing how various conditions affect social influence, you will be in a position to gain the greatest possible success from your efforts to stand for what you believe.

The social influence research study disclosed five areas into which the conditions seem to divide themselves. They are: (1) those conditions having to do with the nature of the problems or situations you are likely to encounter; (2) those concerning the "audience"—the people you are attempting to influence; (3) your home climate; (4) your reputation; and (5) a "service climate." Let us consider them one at a time.

The Problems or Situations

When you first began to study arithmetic back in the early grades of elementary school, you didn't start by trying to solve differential equations or prove geometric theorems. You first had to learn the basic skills of mathematics by solving simple problems. The same principle holds true in the area of social influence. If you attempt to tackle problems you haven't yet acquired the skills to handle, your chances of success are very poor. The basic rule in learning the social influence skills, as in learning any other set of skills, is to *start with the simple problems first*. Here are some general guidelines which may help:

1. Situations involving social problems are easier to handle than those dealing with personal problems.

2. Problems of physical danger seem to be easier than those involving hurt feelings. For example:

LEARN
THE
SIMPLE
SKILLS
FIRST

PROBLEMS + SKILLS = INFLUENCE

1 + 2 = 3

We were coming back from a basketball game, and the boy driving the car was being somewhat reckless. After repeated skidding turns and high speeds, I became quite worried. Finally, I told the driver that I didn't appreciate his driving and would rather walk than run the risk of an accident.

When I said that, all of the others in the car joined in with me and complained about his driving. Upon finding out that the boys didn't like his showing off, the boy slowed down and drove safely.

3. Situations in which there is high "cost-difficulty" (remember that term from Chapter One?) or those requiring much personal sacrifice on your part are more likely to prove successful than situations requiring less effort. This is that same paradoxical-sounding principle we discussed earlier in talking about convictions.

4. When it is obvious to all concerned that you do not stand to gain anything personally from your efforts to influence others, you will be much more successful than if you have some selfish motive, or if the person or persons you are trying to influence *think* you have a selfish motive.

The "Audience"

To say that the nature of the group or individuals you are trying to influence plays an important part in the success or failure of your efforts may seem obvious and just plain common sense. But often it is the "obvious" things—the ones we take the most for granted—which turn out to be crucial factors. What then did we find out about the "audience"?

1. In the first place, the evidence indicates that you are more likely to be successful when you try to influence members of your own sex than those of the opposite sex. This may come as a disappointment to those who feel they are "irresistible" and, therefore, highly influential with the opposite gender.

2. It is easier to carry social influence with your peers (those of your own age), and with those who share your interests and goals than people with whom you have less in common. Here is an everyday example:

> When I got off the bus on the way to school with my friends, I noticed that there was a new girl starting to walk down the street by herself. I thought that since we all were going to the same school we should walk together and get acquainted. I told my friends we should get acquainted with her and they agreed. I knew they all must have wanted to but were afraid to speak up and say so. By being the one to speak up, I, and my girl friends, had made a new friend. We talked with her all the way to school and found out a lot about her. I think it made her happier, too, to know that she had some new friends.

What are some implications of this finding? For one thing, it means that the more you widen your range of interests, the more you will be widening your range of possible influence. For example, if your only interest is in art, the area of your most effective social influence will likely be limited to other artists or appreciators of art.

CAUTION: Do not interpret this finding as an excuse not to try to excel in some field. Each person needs to find one or two things he can do reasonably well in order to fulfill his need for achievement. Also, the great artists, the great musicians, the great scientists are, by and large, people who have become highly specialized. What the research is saying is that a teenager with a "one-track mind" is limited in his influence simply because the breadth of his contacts with other people will be very limited. Therefore, the more conversant you are in different areas, the greater will be your circle of possible influence.

A similar indicator of importance in this finding concerns the age level with which you are most likely to find influence. Right now, probably you feel the most "at home" with other teen-agers. With them you can relax and be yourself, without feeling it necessary to "put on airs" to make what you hope will be a good impression. In other words, you are more likely to be completely sincere with other teen-agers than with younger or older age groups. This sincerity enables you to carry more significant influence with them. Do you see, then, how your influence could be multiplied by gradually enlarging the age range with which you can feel at ease and be your sincere self?

3. Here is one of the more obvious findings: You are more likely to be successful with people you know —friends and classmates—than with strangers. Like the previous finding, this one has a very clear implication: The wider you expand your circle of friends and acquaintances, the more extensive will be your possible social influence.

4. Despite the frequent news stories about mobs and "mob psychology," your chances of carrying effective social influence are much better with organized groups, such as clubs and other school and church groups, than with disorganized mobs or miscellaneous crowds of people.

5. If you are a boy, the evidence suggests that you will probably find you are better able to carry influence with *groups* of other people than with just one individual. The situation is the opposite for girls, who tend to be more effective when they are trying to influence only one person at a time.

Your Home Climate

How do you get along with your brothers and sisters? What sort of relationship do you have with your parents? You may wonder what these questions have to do with your effectiveness in carrying social influence. Would it surprise you to know that the skill with which you are able to handle *home* situations has a direct bearing on your ability to carry social influence outside the home? The teen-agers who are the most effective in standing for their convictions against social pressure are those who seem to have what might be called "peace at home." Learning to solve problems of social conflict among members of your family serves as good practice and training for meeting similar situations outside the home. The family dinner table is a very important forum for discussing problems of social pressure.

Here is an example of a teen-ager who is learning the value of the home as a laboratory in which to try out skills for carrying effective social influence:

My brother and sister were just recovering from being sick when my mother had to go away. She asked me to take care of them and try to keep them quiet. Shortly after she left, they began running around the house and screaming. Telling them to be quiet would do no good, so I got them interested in playing a game my brother had gotten for Christmas. Although I kept them quiet and interested, I missed a television program I had been looking forward to seeing.

MAGNETIC
LINES
OF
FORCE

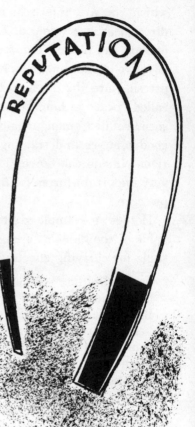

Your Reputation

The field of labor-management relations offers striking examples of the effectiveness of reputation in carrying social influence. It is not unusual for the representatives of the employees of an individual factory or, perhaps, of a group of factories such as all steelworkers or auto workers, to find themselves in disagreement with the representatives of the management side of the company or industry. Often, the viewpoints of the two sides are so far apart that the only thing upon which they agree is that they cannot agree! At this point, strike votes are taken and threats are made by both sides. In the midst of these sometimes very bitter and seemingly "impossible" situations, a professional arbitrator is brought in to talk with both sides.

In an amazing number of cases, the arbitrator is able to work out acceptable conditions in a very short time and, in practically all cases, he is eventually able to negotiate a peaceful settlement of differences. Why is he successful where other intelligent men had failed? One of the major reasons is that both labor and management *expect* him to be able to find a solution to their problems. In other words, he has a *reputation* for being able to solve such disputes. Thus, the representatives of both sides are much more receptive to *his* suggestions than they might be to the same suggestions made by someone they did not recognize as being an "expert" at arbitrating disputes of this type.

You can use this same principle in your own efforts. If you are recognized by your friends and others your age as being the kind of person who is not afraid to stand for his convictions, and who is able to see both sides of an issue before coming to conclusions, your chances of success are greatly enhanced.

How do you get such a reputation? You get it in exactly the same manner that you acquire any other type of reputation—one step at a time. In this case, you start with just one small act of influence. Then you use what you learned from that experience to help you in the next situation. The combined knowledge you have thus obtained is applied to yet a third "problem," and so forth. To be sure, you will not be fully successful *every* time you attempt to carry influence, any more than the arbitrator is completely successful every time he tries to negotiate a labor-management dispute. But if you start with the simple problems first, and remember the social influence skills outlined in this book, the experiences of other teen-agers indicate that you will be successful a substantial part of the time. Eventually, you will acquire a reputation of standing up for what you believe that will make you even more effective in your efforts.

Cultivating a "Service Climate"

One of the best means of preparing the way for more effective social influence is through the cultivation of what might be called a "service climate." This concept is closely connected to the matter of reputation. It involves being sensitive to the needs and feelings of others—cultivating "the art of being imposed upon" in your daily relationships.

The influence that grows out of such service comes about indirectly. That is, you do not perform the act of service in order to influence the other person. You do it out of a deep concern for his needs and a desire to be helpful. But because you do serve him, you thereby create a favorable climate for social influence. Here is an example:

Yesterday I sort of took over the baseball department in my neighborhood, yet quite accidentally. I was just hitting pop-ups and fliers to myself when the little boy from across the street came to watch. Realizing that his mother probably didn't want him to play in the street, I came to the conclusion that I was setting a bad example, so I offered to play with him in his front yard. Several times the ball went into the road, but I managed to get the idea into his head that he shouldn't be in the street at all. After a while, though, the other small fries in the neighborhood wanted to get into the act, so we moved to a backyard and really got into some baseball experiences that will, I hope, last in their minds as the true meaning of baseball.

When this young man went out to practice baseball, he didn't do it to be of service or to carry social influence. He was simply having fun and getting some exercise. The younger child might have been considered an intruder by some teen-agers and told, "Beat it, kid, I'm busy!" Instead, this boy saw an opportunity to be of service and followed through on it. In doing so, he not only taught an object lesson in safety, but laid a foundation for exerting positive influence in the future. Which teen-ager do you think would have the better chance of influencing small children—the one who says, "Beat it, kid, I'm busy!" or the one who, like the boy in this true incident, creates a "service climate"?

Action!

You can start right now to develop this sort of climate in your own life. First, ask yourself this question, "What do I have to offer in service to others? What skills do I possess that might possibly be of use to someone else?" List them on a sheet of paper. (Don't forget such "intangible" skills as making friends easily or being able to think through problems clearly to the best decision.)

In what types of situations are you the most likely to be able to use these skills in the service of others? Do you know of an individual situation in which you

can be of service *right now?* Make a step-by-step plan
to *do* something about it *now.*

One girl who made good grades in algebra gave up
her favorite evening television programs on weekends
to help her friend better understand the subject. A
boy took it upon himself to do yard work in the summer
and snow shoveling in the winter for an elderly couple
who lived on his block, and did it without pay. *What
can you do?*

IN A NUTSHELL

*There are certain conditions that can go
a long way toward determining the success or failure of your attempts to stand
up for what you believe. These conditions
fall into five general categories:*

*1. The nature of the problem or situa-
tion. Start with the problems that are
easier to handle at first. For example, social problems are easier than personal
problems, and situations involving physical danger are easier than those having to
do with "hurt feelings."*

*2. The nature of the "audience"—the
person or persons you are trying to influence. You will probably find it easier to
influence members of your own sex than
those of the opposite sex. Boys seem to do*

73

better with groups, while girls tend to be more successful with individuals. You will have more influence with people your own age than with other age levels, and with people you know rather than with strangers. Common interests are also important. Organized groups are much more promising fields for social influence than disorganized mobs.

3. How well you get along at home is an important factor in determining how effective you are outside the home.

4. If you can develop a reputation for standing for your convictions, you will be much more influential.

5. By constantly being alert to possibilities for rendering genuine service to others you will be creating a climate conducive to carrying social influence.

CHAPTER THREE

The Keys to Your Personal Power

The
Keys
to Your
Personal Power

From convictions and conditions we move now to consider the actual keys, or skills, that can enable you to be much more effective in standing up for what you believe. In order that you will not get "indigestion" from trying to swallow all of them at once, they have been divided into five "chewable bites" or categories. They are: (1) perceptual skills; (2) skills and characteristics of personality; (3) skills of "image-building"; (4) general skills; and (5) skills of evaluation.

Action!

Just reading through the skills will have no more effect on your life than looking at a display of weapons will make you a good shot! In order for you to really *learn* some of these skills, you must approach the task systematically, taking one step at a time. First, go through the entire Chapter Three, reading only the headings, the subheadings, and the words in italics. This will give you a quick idea of the social influence skills at your command. Then select the *one category* which you feel could contribute the most to your own ability to stand for your convictions. It may be the Perceptual Skills, the Skills of "Image-Building," or one of the other three categories. When you have completed this, go back once again to that section, read it through in its entirety, then select the *one skill* from that category which you feel you have the best chance of developing right now to a high degree. Then write down on a sheet of paper *one thing* you can do during the coming week to practice that skill. Put down in detail just *how* you are going to do this. For the next six or seven days, follow through on your plan, and at the end of the week write down what happened. To what extent were you successful? What evidence do you have to support that opinion? What can you do the next week in order to improve your skill? By following this scientific approach to learning these skills, you will be amazed how much more effective you become in social pressure situations. The teen-agers who supplied those thousands of true incidents have shown that these skills of social influence really work if they are given half a chance!

After you feel you have that first skill down pat, come back to this chapter again and select another one to try. In this way you can increase the number and variety of your skills of social influence, thereby making certain that you will be "prepared for anything."

Perceptual Skills

One of the most important groups of skills for carrying social influence and, indeed, for living at all with other people, is what we call "perceptual skills." What do we mean by perceptual skills? In general, they have to do with developing your social sensitivity—your awareness of and appreciation for the thoughts, feelings, and attitudes of others. Admittedly, these are difficult skills to master. When man is born, he is an animal creature, seeking only to satisfy his own basic needs and desires. Some people never rise above this infantile stage in their attitudes. But because man is man and not some lower animal, he has the capacity to sense others' feelings, to go beyond his animal nature, as it were, and to take pleasure in the satisfactions and achievements of others. The extent to which an individual is able thus to deny himself for the sake of others is one of the commonly used measurements of maturity.

It can be safely said that few of us develop to a high degree whatever capacity we may have for social sensitivity. It is precisely because achieving a high level of social perception is difficult and because acts of true selflessness are comparatively rare that the skills of perception are so effective in carrying social influence.

You will encounter the term "ego-involved attitude" a number of times in the pages ahead. An ego-involved attitude is an idea which one holds so strongly, and which is so important to his feelings of security, that any questioning of its value or truth is regarded by him as a threat to his personality. In response to such a threat, people usually become defensive and argumentative. When this happens, the doors of the mind snap shut, just as the doors of a fort are slammed shut by soldiers when an invasion is threatened. With the "receiving channels" to the mind thus closed off, the reception of new or different ideas is very difficult, if not impossible. Thus, social influence, or any influence at all, with persons who have had their ego-involved attitudes threatened or challenged is almost out of the question. By being aware of this, and developing a sensitivity to other people's ego-involved attitudes, you can "keep the channels open" and thus greatly improve your chances of working with them effectively.

Of course, each of us has some attitudes in which

he is ego-involved to a greater or lesser degree. One of the most difficult aspects of dealing with this problem is that we often have no way of knowing when we might hit one of these sensitive spots in our personal relationships. For instance, you probably never give a second thought to how tall you are, simply accepting your height as something you cannot do anything about. But have you ever had the experience of casually mentioning stature in the course of a conversation with friends, to find out suddenly that one of them is very sensitive about his height, or lack of it? If the words, "Oh, I didn't mean anything personal," seem to come out frequently in your conversations, you probably have an unusual "talent" for stepping on people's ego-involved attitudes. Following are some skills and suggestions which might help you in this often perplexing area of human relations.

1. *Try to discover what a situation means in terms of the other person's personality before attempting to apply a moral principle.* It will help you to know, if possible, the extent to which he is ego-involved in the situation. A superficial application of principle without personal insight is very seldom effective. Here is an example:

> When a fellow at school was going with a former girl friend of mine, he treated me very nastily because she still smiled at me. I kept returning his remarks in a soft voice or just remained still, try-

81

ing to be his friend. When he still did not change, I got disgusted. One day I returned one of his remarks the way he gave it out. I almost fought him because I lost my temper. Time has made us forget our anger, but we will never be friends.

2. *Scolding, sarcasm, "getting even," and unkind stories that violate the ego-involved attitudes of others will severely limit your chances of carrying much social influence with them.* This is a negative skill (something *not* to do), but an extremely important one. The following incident from an earlier part of this book bears repeating because it illustrates this principle very well.

My group of friends were planning a drinking party and I felt they were wrong. I got quite angry and told them off. I told them that drinking was a cheap thrill and I felt they should have more respect for themselves than to go around drinking at fifteen and sixteen just to be big. They called me a prude and stuck up. I told them as long as they went through with it I wanted no part of them.

We must at least give this girl credit for having the courage to stand up for her convictions! Many teen-agers would have silently "gone along with the crowd." But how much more effective she would have been if she had stopped to consider the fact that the other teen-agers were very much ego-involved in the situation. Apparently, they thought that drinking and having drinking parties was a sign that they were "grown up" and no longer subject to their parents' rules and the laws of society. By scolding them as a parent might scold a naughty child, she made them defensive, they closed their minds, and any hope for effective social influence vanished.

Family relationships is an area in which the lack of this skill often causes friction. Here is an example:

> The situation had to do with my brother. There was something I thought he should have done. He didn't do it, so I criticized him sharply. It only made for a bad situation. My brother became antagonistic and more bitter to doing what I thought he should. He never did it!

3. *When you feel it necessary to criticize, do it in a constructive manner that will not embarrass the other individual, and will allow him to "save face."* This is an important technique for "keeping the channels open." One of the most common types of situations in which this skill can be especially useful finds a girl riding in a car with a boy who tries to show off by demonstrating how fast he can go around corners and how close he can come to other cars without hitting them. If the girl wants to keep his friendship (as well as a whole skin), she must find a way to get him to act sensibly, without making him too painfully conscious that he has been acting like a fool. This can sometimes be done by appealing to another of his ego-involved attitudes,

such as his manly pride in being the "protector" of the girl.

Here is a good example of this skill in action at a basketball game:

The scene was one of our recent high school basketball games. Our team was doing substantially well on the basketball floor, but on the bench, where I happened to be, team unity was going to the dogs. The general feeling was that after a hard week of practice, we all deserved something more than the bench on Friday night. After realizing that this attitude could seriously damage team morale, I decided to do what I could about it. I noticed that a great deal of the contempt was originating with the player seated next to me and I mentioned to him in as nonchalant a manner as possible, "You know, just being able to see a game like this makes practicing seem really worthwhile."

He didn't say anything for about a minute, but when the team came down the floor he began cheering the team in as vigorous and earnest a manner as I have ever seen.

Combining your criticism with a sincere compliment or with some observation about a good quality of the individual is a very good technique for helping him to "save face." Here is an example having to do with the problem of race prejudice:

I have a friend who is prejudiced against the Negro race. She often used the words "nigger" and "jig-a-boo." One day I said, "I like you a lot and I respect you and I hope you respect me, and if you do, you will refrain from using (the above) words." She hasn't used these words in my presence again. We now are much better friends and she is learning how to get along with Negroes better.

And here is an example of how the lack of this skill makes social influence almost impossible:

At a p.j. party the discussion turned to a group of about twenty-five boys in school who, although they are all very nice, have lately indulged in a great deal of smoking and a considerable amount of drinking. Everyone was talking about it, and the general consensus of opinion seemed to be that it wasn't *really* so bad. I said that although I, too, thought the boys were real sharp and had lots of potential, I was very disappointed in their recent actions and had lost a lot of respect for them. I then discussed some of the members individually.

Because of the fact that I discussed individuals, I failed completely. Many of the group resented it and when the boys found out, I was completely ostracized. My whole purpose was then lost and I had cut all immediate hopes for any action.

4. *If you can help to build self-respect in the other person or persons, this will be a great help in carrying social influence.* Self-confidence is the key to self-respect. If you have no confidence in your own abilities

or ideas, you will have little respect for yourself. The same is true of others. Therefore, the chief questions become, "How can you help to build this person's confidence? What do you know about him that will give you some clue to his ability? In what area or areas does he have some competence to which you can appeal and upon which you can help him build?" In other words, accentuate the positive; look for the good qualities rather than the bad.

The boy who wrote the following incident was using this skill to good purpose, though some might question his way of doing it. Does "the end justify the means" in this case?

I was on the tennis courts not too long ago, and I was playing with a boy who is deaf. He has had a very serious operation on his legs, and another factor is that his parents are broken up. He is one of the nicest guys one can meet, but he is very sad in his life. I felt sorry for him, and he wants to become a great tennis player by practicing it. So I sympathized with him and let him beat me, which really built up his confidence, and you would never know how happy he was. It was great for him. Please don't think that I am a real good tennis player because I'm not; it is only that I have played longer than he has. This principle I did goes along with my idea, "It is better to give than it is to receive."

Persons who engage in foolish behavior often do so because they do not feel sure of themselves. Their behavior is a kind of "cover-up" for their lack of confidence. By helping them to increase their self-confidence, you will be doing them a real service and, at the same time, laying the groundwork for possible influence, like the girl in this incident.

One of my friends got her hair cut from real long to real short. She didn't like it at first, and felt that no one else did, either. We were supposed to have a picnic at a lake with a bunch of the kids that weekend, and Judy wasn't going to go because of her hair. I told her that she was silly, and she was being ridiculous. She said she didn't want to go and be made a fool of. I told her she cared too much what other people thought of her and certainly was carrying this too far. "You're you, and your friends like you for the way you act, not the way your hair is cut. Besides, you haven't given anyone a chance to like it, and you're saying they don't. Now quit this talk, be yourself, and go!" She went.

NOTE: These girls were obviously very good friends. If they had not been, the "scolding" approach which was used in the incident might very well have backfired. As has been pointed out, this is generally *not* a very good way to influence others.

Here is a very important point regarding the matter of self-respect: The evidence produced by the teen-agers in the study of social influence indicated conclusively that *you cannot gain either self-respect or the respect of others by violating your own moral prin-*

ciples to gain "popularity." Such influence as you may seem to gain by doing so will be of a short-lived variety and, in the long run, you will have earned nothing but contempt. Girls often find themselves under great social pressure to compromise their moral standards. They fall prey to a deceptive argument used by some socially ambitious girls as an excuse and by some totally selfish boys as a "lever." This argument goes something like this: "Let's be realistic. In this day and age if you want to be popular and not left sitting at home on date nights, you have to be willing to let go a little—let the boy have his way." The number of girls who, to their sorrow, discover the fallacy of this argument runs into the thousands every year!

5. *"Putting yourself in the other person's shoes"— trying to see the issue from his point of view—is one of the most effective skills for overcoming prejudice and intolerance.* After all, prejudice consists of other people's behavior *as seen by you*, not by them. One seldom sees himself as being prejudiced or intolerant or as possessing any other undesirable trait. Simply pointing out his prejudice to the other person, then, will not result in very effective influence, except of a negative kind. On the contrary, the more you learn to step into the other's shoes mentally and try to look at the situation from his viewpoint, the more effective you will be in dealing with problems of this type. Here are some examples:

PERCEPTUAL SKILLS

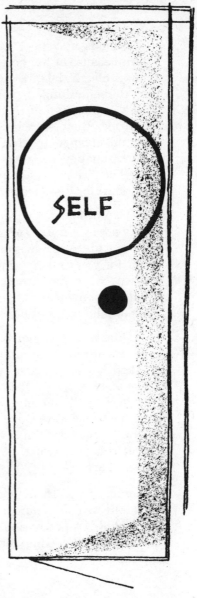

SELF

SEE BEYOND

Friends at school were laughing at a foreign girl, because of her accent. I knew this was wrong and, though the girls were my friends, I felt I had to do something. I pointed out to them, should they suddenly find themselves sent to a school in Europe, their speech would be hard and would sound strange to the European children. Also, how unhappy they would be, too, when laughed at. The girls seem to understand, and I think they are showing more respect.

Two of my girl friends were talking about the way a new girl dressed. I knew this was wrong. So I went up to the girls and said, "I don't think it's fair for you to be talking about her. Maybe in the town she comes from, they dress like that." I guess I convinced them, because I have not heard them talking about her again.

During homeroom period, one day last week, James decided he would hide Bill's books and asked if I would hand them to him. I thought it would be a good joke so I did. But just a short while later I put myself in the place of the boy whose books were being hidden. So I went and got James and told him my feelings. He also decided that this was wrong. So he got the books and put them back.

Summing up, then, you will find that among the most effective of your social influence skills can be these skills of perception—learning to be sensitive to the needs and feelings of others. Try a few of them and see!

Skills and Characteristics of Personality

High on most lists of the qualities of "my ideal boy," or "my ideal girl" is one that declares ". . . must have a nice personality." Aside from the fact that probably no two persons would agree on exactly what constitutes a "nice personality," this phrase demonstrates that in most minds the word "personality" projects a picture of charm and warm friendliness, of someone who is easy to know and nice to have around. Actually, the word is much broader than that. Person-ality has to do with the *whole person*, the sum total of all that is you. This includes such things as your habits and attitudes. The social skills study found that some of these aspects of your personality have an important bearing upon your ability to carry significant social influence. Three of them deserve special mention here.

1. *You are more likely to carry social influence if your behavior is best described as "direct action."* That is, once you have decided upon a course of action, you should carry it through without hesitation—firmly, thoughtfully, but calmly. This does not mean that you put your head down and charge blindly into the fray! You cannot see where you are going very well with your head down! You must keep your eyes open and be alert to any necessity to change your plans or approach. But you will be much more effective if it is clear that you intend to follow up your convictions.

There is nothing very inspiring about the "wishy-washy" sort of person who seems to change direction with every shift of the winds of public opinion.

Here is a young man who tried to follow through with direct action, in spite of the kidding of his friends.

A while ago we were asked to write our philosophy of life in class. Some of the kids wrote a couple of sentences and then stopped. As I was writing my second page, these kids began to kid me. But I kept going because I figured that the people who asked us to do it wanted the best job we could do, and I was trying to give it to them.

2. *An important skill in social influence is developing the habit of liking people.* If you think that most people are not likable, it is probably because you have not taken the time to get to know them very well. Here is a little technique that might help you: Make a list of about ten things that you think you would like to know about a person, such as name, occupation, hobbies, ideas, philosophy of life, and so forth. Memorize the list. Then when you meet a new person, try to find out these things, and you will discover that almost everyone is interesting and likable to some degree. *(A word of caution:* Use discretion in getting your information. People don't like to be interrogated as though they were being booked into jail. Many of the essential facts can be obtained "secondhand" or in an indirect manner.) The young man in the following

incident discovered something new and ended up with a good friend:

> I met someone one time and I thought he was a pretty mean person and wouldn't associate with him. Then one day I had a great disappointment and he came over and told me that everything was O.K. and that I don't have to worry, because there will be chances to do other things better than that. I then saw how good a person he was and he became my best friend.

3. *Those whose personalities make them flexible in social situations carry more social influence than those who are dogmatic and rigid in their reactions.* Be certain that you understand the difference between flexibility and compromising your principles. To be flexible is to maintain an attitude of "this is the way I see the situation from the best information I can get now, but I am always willing to hear new evidence." This is the opposite of the "my mind is made up, so don't confuse me with the facts" attitude. We spoke of this same principle in an earlier section of the book when we were talking about convictions. Nobody likes the kind of person who is always sure he is right and everyone else is wrong. This sort of attitude is almost certain to make any effective social influence impossible, *even though the person who possesses this attitude may be absolutely right.* It is the *attitude* of inflexibility more than what is said, that makes the "know-it-all" a V.U.P. (very undesirable person).

PERSONALITY COUNTS
V.I.P.
VERY INTERESTED PERSON
OR V.U.P.
VERY UNDESIRABLE PERSON

By being flexible, the following boy was able to offer an acceptable solution to a problem that threatened to dissolve a friendship:

In our school orchestra in which I play first violin, my music partner and I have been having a few minor conflicts. Since I am in third chair, and he plays fourth, he is responsible for the music (getting it out, turning pages, and putting it back after completion). However, we haven't been having tryouts nearly as often as we should, and he thought that he had an unfair responsibility. Although I didn't fully agree with him, I knew he should be given a chance. But with several concerts coming up, tryouts are, for the time being, extinct. So I suggested that we merely put it on a cooperative basis, that is, he gets the music out and I put it back.

Here is another excellent example of flexibility (with a generous dose of persistence added for good measure):

When I suggested a change in our church's youth group charter to the president, he pointed out that my change was impractical (as it was then), but he pointed out that the situation I had tried to relieve *was* a problem. I then looked at the problem from a different angle and thought up an easier, more practical solution.

When meetings resume in the fall, a vote will be taken on my change. I am confident that my change will be adopted as I have the sanction of the officers and president. If I hadn't paid attention to him earlier, I wouldn't have had a chance for success.

The Skills of "Image-Building"

Our society is becoming increasingly "image conscious." Vast sums of money and great quantities of time are being spent by individuals and corporations in the attempt to build up a "favorable image" of themselves in the public mind. Corporations do it to sell products. Politicians do it to get votes. And the evidence produced in this study indicates that there are certain skills of "image-building" which you can develop that will make you much more effective in standing for your convictions.

We are not speaking here of just making a superficial "good impression." Persons who concentrate on "putting up a good front" live in the constant fear that some day someone will look behind the exterior and find that, like a movie set, there is little or nothing behind the nice facade.

No, the only "image" that will be of any lasting value to you is the *true* one. Your chief concern, then, should be to make certain that the picture you present to others is a true representation of your thoughts and feelings. This is no easy task, for we almost never see ourselves as others see us. You have undoubtedly had the experience of being completely misunderstood, or of hurting another's feelings when you thought you were paying him a compliment. Such problems of communication are a part of the effort to create a proper image. Here are some specific suggestions.

1. *Try to make the other person realize that you like him.* In doing this, of course, it is essential that you actually *do* like him. (There is no romantic connotation in our use of the word "like.") We have already spoken of the importance of developing the habit of liking people, and suggested a technique to help you do this. Here we are concerned with the problem of making your admiration for people apparent *to them.* The following was written by a boy who had to prove his liking for his friend, even when the friend seemed not to want his friendship:

> I've had one of my best friends fail a grade. After school started again, he tried to keep away from his old classmates. I was his only real friend. Most of his close friends (for years) have moved. His closest friend died with polio this past summer. After his failing, he wanted to lose all contact with me, especially. He would annoy me at school and call me and tell me he was going to make me *hate* him. I went on treating him like nothing had ever happened.
>
> This seemed to have brought him out of the clouds and into the "normal" stride of things. Now he is around the old class, as much as he can be. We have friendly conversations over the telephone now.

If you can be genuinely interested in the activities and interests of others, this is one of the best ways to show your liking for them. In the following incident, the narrator's interest took a negative turn, but it nonetheless showed that she was interested and concerned for her friend.

One of my girl friends at another school is being rushed into some sorority. I tried to tell her how wrong they are and, also, they are against the law. When she entered the school, she and her parents signed a statement saying she would not join a sorority, and if she pledged she would be calling her parents and herself liars.

It was today I talked with her, so I can't report any real results. However, she promised to talk with some of the other girls who were being rushed, and present the "cons" of joining, as I had.

Another effective way to demonstrate your regard for a person is to show that you have respect for him, for his ideas and convictions. You cannot accomplish this with a "holier than thou" or "smarter than thou" attitude, which this teen-ager found out in a youth meeting.

Last Sunday there was an MYF meeting on the subject, "Has Science Found God?" with three experts making up a symposium. Now I was chairman of this group and the meeting, but I took the role of a pessimist, I'm afraid, and perhaps did not do as much as I could have. As chairman, my job was to keep the meeting going, not to interject my opinions. This experience was a social influence all right, but certainly not a positive one. I know that I can still profit from it. There were many things I automatically objected to and many I defended throughout the duration of the meeting. I think that many members were discouraged from attempting to say anything, fearing that they might be contradicted.

If you had been a member of this youth group, what do you think would have been this person's chances of carrying any social influence with you after his performance at the meeting?

2. *As with most other aspects of social influence, building a favorable image is best accomplished one step at a time.* Your image is largely a matter of the reputation you achieve, and we have already pointed out that this is built gradually, a step at a time.

A good example of this technique in action concerns the student who is having trouble with his grades. His parents might "lay down the law" and demand that the next time his report card had better show all "A's," even though this might mean jumping from failure to the top in one big step! As any student knows, this is practically impossible to do. However if the parents would say instead, "We want you to bring each grade up one step during this next report period," this the student might be more realistically expected to do. In the following incident, the boy was able to carry important social influence because he gradually built up an image of tolerance.

A friend of mine is in the hospital. His "roommate" is prejudiced. Many of the nurses are colored. At first, this roommate was a little reluctant to cooperate. But after two days he was good friends with all the nurses. I felt this is due to him seeing my friend always friendly and having fun.

CAUTION! As you may have found from painful personal experience, it often takes only one thoughtless act or one "slip of the tongue" to shatter a reputation or an image you may have worked months or years to establish.

3. *Appealing to a good image others have of themselves is very effective.* Each of us likes to think well of himself. Thus, we tend to react positively to those who give us opportunities to show ourselves in a favorable light. For example, a girl asked a boy in a group to make the other boys behave during the meeting. This implied his ability to do so, and got results. Making others feel wanted or needed and asking them for advice are other illustrations of this same technique. Here is another example:

The teacher left the room and put a boy in charge of the class. I think this boy stood up for his beliefs by telling the class to be quiet. As a result, the class behaved very well.

If you can change another person's self-image, you can often change his related behavior. One teen-age boy objected to piano lessons because "they are sissy." When he was invited to play at a school pep rally, however, he saw himself and his piano skills in a quite different light.

General Skills

There were a number of skills of social influence which didn't seem to fit into any "pattern," but which are nonetheless important. We shall simply call them "general skills" and enumerate them here.

1. *When you are attempting to influence a group of people, you will be much more successful if you can have at least one other person on your side before you start.* Ideally, of course, this one other person would be the leader of the group. Perhaps there is someone in the group whom you know shares your basic conviction but has been afraid to speak out. This sort of situation was dramatically illustrated when a group of junior high school boys from a "good neighborhood" were arrested for vandalism. As the police questioned them individually, each boy stated that he knew what they were doing was wrong, and that he did not want to do it, but that all the rest of the boys did. If just *one* of those boys had spoken out and said, "I don't think we should do this," it never would have happened and those boys would not now have police rec-

ords to haunt them the rest of their lives.

2. This example leads into the next skill. *When faced with an undesirable action, try to suggest an alternative, more desirable action.* There is sound psychology behind this skill. The motivation *not* to do something is not nearly so great as the motivation to *do* something positive. Here is how this principle might work out in a cheating situation:

> A boy in one of my classes had the reputation for cheating. I knew he was smart enough to be able to do the work, so without mentioning cheating I spent a little time each day studying with him, making sure he knew his lesson. I think that has stopped his cheating and he is regaining friends that he lost when he cheated.

This is one of the best possible skills for getting yourself out of those potentially embarrassing or dangerous social situations. And it is something you can prepare for in advance by anticipating such possible situations and then thinking of some reasonable and attractive alternatives.

An important added note to this skill concerns the matter of timing. If the alternative action can be suggested *before* the undesirable action starts, your chances of influence are much better. Remember that old rule of physics: A body (or group of bodies, as the case may be) once in motion tends to remain in motion. It is much easier to change the direction of that motion before action starts. Here are examples:

One day a group of my friends were talking about a teacher they disliked and how they were going to drop books at a certain time. I started talking about a test we were going to have. They forgot about dropping the books.

In my fundamental speech class there is a boy in front of me who often bothers the class. Yesterday when we were talking about a speech, he started bothering the kids about him. I gave him a trick puzzle to solve. This kept him busy and only took a short time to show him. He worked on the puzzle instead of bothering the class and I feel I learned more this way than if he had continued bothering the class.

Through our four years of high school we plan and work toward one goal—a senior trip—and everyone goes. We held a class meeting to lay some of the necessary plans, and to outline the possible trips and modes of transportation. We were deciding between train and bus; since last year's trip by bus has been implanted in students' minds, this was the general opinion: train, by all means. Since I felt the bus "angle" should be considered, I stated some of the good features and why I thought we should go by bus. Since I was on the trip committee, I also presented some things which our chairman had hastily gone over. As it turned out, many others were considering the bus, but only needed a leader. Thus I found support for my ideas.

When the suggested desirable action is of such a nature as to bring out the best talents of other people, social influence is far more probable than when this is not the case.

The other day my Dad was very concerned because I hadn't received a C average in my school subjects the last six weeks. He didn't think that I had applied myself to the best of my ability, especially in English. He decided that he would make a list of activities that I would discontinue, with my approval, so I would have more time to study.

At first I was mad because he had discovered that I wasn't applying myself. I later realized that he was helping me see that the only way I would get to college next year was to work now. I have dropped my social activities and time-consuming hobbies to make time so I can study. I have a goal to make the honor roll, which I hope I can fulfill. I am glad that he cared enough about my education to point up this fallacy in my studies.

3. *Make your idealism realistic.* Teen-agers are naturally very idealistic. They develop great hopes and dreams, and cannot seem to wait for the day when they will go out "to save the world." For the most part, this is as it should be. Most of the great improvements in our society have been made by men and women of vision and idealism. But they are persons *who have learned to make their idealism realistic*! Those who

preach an idealism which is impossible in our social environment have as little influence as those whose "realism" makes them abandon their ideals.

We have pointed out previously that, while it may be true that over-idealism without a realistic base is seldom very effective in carrying social influence, the solution to the problem is *not* one of hasty compromise or total capitulation. A boy, for instance, wants his girl to be beyond reproach, and does not respect her when she compromises her standards.

4. *Learn to be an "observant listener."* The skills of good listening are often more difficult to achieve than those of good speaking. When you are in a group, observe carefully the relationships among the members of the group. This knowledge can add greatly to your social influence potential. When dealing with individuals, it is correspondingly important to really *listen* to what they have to say, not just be *hearing* their words.

5. *Know when to talk and when not to talk.* This skill is closely connected with the previous one. The perennial "talker" who monopolizes the discussion is not very likely to carry much influence. Those who make the greatest contribution to discussions are the persons who listen until they have had time to organize their thoughts, rather than making impulsive and frequent interjections. A good device to use in this context is what is called the "speak third" principle. Once

you have made a contribution to the discussion, wait until at least two others have said something before you make another comment.

Timing is a very important related skill here. Sometimes our words don't seem to be heard by anyone simply because we say the right thing, but at the wrong time. The following girl apparently chose the right time:

> My girl friend was very anxious to get her driver's license so that she could have the car on Saturdays. She has her license now and last Saturday her dad said she could use the car if she drove her mother and brother around first. She complained because she had to do this. I pointed out that she had wanted her license and now she could use the car when she finished driving her family around. She realized that she was getting her wish (to use the car) and drove her family willingly so she could use it.

6. *Use the opinions of respected authorities to give weight to your statements.* Debaters and other public speakers use this technique very effectively. If you can say "So-and-so says this" (when "so-and-so" is someone whom the people you are trying to influence recognize as an outstanding authority or as a person of some stature), it carries much more weight than when you simply give your own opinion against someone else's. The more authoritative the evidence you can produce for your stand, the more effective will be your influence.

INFLUENCE

REFLECTS

YOUR TRUE

IMAGE

7. *Set an example for others to follow.* "Do as I say, not as I do" is the weakest of arguments. Whether the item in question is civil rights, cheating on exams, or the proper conduct on a date, nothing speaks louder than quiet example. To paraphrase Ralph Waldo Emerson, what you *are* speaks so loud people cannot hear what you *say!* The boy in this incident discovered the power of one small example:

> I was driving down the street and was courteous to another driver, not because it was the right thing to do, but because I was feeling good. I ended up following the person I was courteous to. The driver of the other car was courteous to someone else. This started a chain reaction . . . and made everyone happy.

Try it yourself!

8. *Form the habit of generalizing on your actions.* This means that if you are successful in carrying social influence in a certain kind of situation, you should try to think of other situations in which the same techniques might work. Do the same if you are unsuccessful, and you will be able to avoid possible frustration and failure in the future. This is a form of evaluation. You will find more on this subject a little further in this book.

9. *Actions you carry out because of "the principle of the thing" or "to stand up for your rights" are often*

petty, and they hardly ever influence others effectively.
We have been saying all along that you *should* have
principles and that you *should* be willing to stand for
them. Are we now contradicting that? Definitely not!
What we are reporting here is one of the important
findings from the social influence study—when your
only reason for doing something is because of "the
principle of the thing," you are likely using the word
"principle" as a kind of crutch to try to support an
otherwise very shaky argument. The point of this negative skill, then, is to make very sure that a *genuine*
principle is involved, and that it is worth standing for,
before you use this timeworn phrase as a reason for
taking (or not taking) action. The same can be said
for "standing up for your rights." Most "rights" are
privileges which must be earned. Therefore, make certain you have earned them and your influence will be
much greater.

Here is an example of stubbornness in the disguise
of "principle":

> In February our school music department put
> on the musical, *Oklahoma.* I was collecting tickets
> at the door. My mother had purchased three
> tickets in advance the previous week, but she had
> lost the coin purse containing them. When our
> family came to see *Oklahoma* she explained the
> situation to me and asked if they could get in
> without tickets. I reviewed the situation very
> hurriedly and in a snap decision I said "No!" be-

cause I didn't think it would be right to let some-body in without letting everyone in who didn't have their tickets.

As a result, I made her buy three more tickets at the door, making a grand total of six tickets the family needed to get in. After weighing the facts of the situation, I feel that my snap decision was very unjust and thoughtless because they had already paid for their tickets the previous week.

10. *Plan ahead!* All of us have been amused by those "plan ahead" signs that run out of space. But the lack of planning in trying to carry social influence is no laughing matter. We have suggested at several points the importance of trying to anticipate possible social pressure situations and preparing yourself in advance to meet them. Most of these situations *can* be pre-dicted. Few teen-agers are so naïve that they are to-tally surprised when they find themselves facing im-portant moral decisions, for example. *And it is very often too late to start looking for a "way out" when these high-pressure situations present themselves.*

Action!

Look at your list of convictions once again. Select the five convictions which in your opinion have the most important moral implications for you. Write each one across the top of a separate sheet of paper. Draw a line down the middle of each sheet under the conviction, dividing the space into left and right halves. Over the left-hand column, write "Situations," and head the right-hand one "Skills." Now list under "Situations" the types of situations in which each conviction is the most likely to be challenged. Use the back of the sheet or extra paper, if necessary. Naturally, you will not be able to anticipate *every* possible situation, but you will know enough of them to get into the habit of planning ahead. You will also find that having thought through these situations will make it easier to think of ways of handling new ones.

Now, in the right-hand column, opposite each situation, make a notation as to the action you think would be the most appropriate to meet that situation, and the social skills involved in such action. Is there a phrase or sentence embodying those skills which you can make a part of your mental "tool kit," to be used in "emergencies"? For example, one boy found that the phrase, "Ah, that's kid stuff!" made an effective prefix to suggesting alternative actions when he was with a group of boys. If someone suggested stealing hubcaps "for kicks," he would exclaim, "Ah, that's kid stuff! Let's go over to my house and get something to eat." Here he was using at least two very effective "weapons." He was appealing to a favorable self-image (they preferred to think of themselves as "men," not "kids"), and he was suggesting a desirable alternative *before the undesirable activity got started.* In this way, he was able to carry effective influence and still retain the friendship of "the gang." In her fine book, *Love and the Facts of Life,** Dr. Evelyn Millis Duvall suggests that girls should develop little techniques like this for handling "over-amorous" dates. One girl found that "Ooooh, please, you are too much for me!" (followed, perhaps, by the suggestion, "Maybe you'd better take me home") was effective with most "Don Juans." Another used a touch of humor as she removed an offending hand with the surprised comment, "Why, this isn't Tuesday, is it?" (Of course, it was never "Tuesday." On Tuesdays, she used another day of the week!) For those more insistent "Romeos," still another girl reaches over, turns on the ignition, and says sweetly, "Will you drive, or shall I?" Whatever techniques or skills you use, the important thing is *"Plan Ahead."*

---

*New York: Association Press, 1963.

Skills of Evaluation

Just as the most effective teen-agers were those who planned ahead, so it was found that "looking back" was also important for continued success. Such evaluation is a part of the "scientific" approach to learning the skills of social influence as it was outlined in the beginning of this section. Evaluation of some kind is absolutely essential to progress in almost any endeavor. Through this technique you can determine whether or not you are really "getting anywhere," why you are or are not doing so, and what you might do to improve. Here are some suggestions for helping you to evaluate your own efforts.

1. *The method of "characteristic differences."* This is a very useful technique that will enable you to see just which skills are the most effective for you, and why. This method will also make it possible for you to predict in advance your probable chances of success in a given type of social-pressure situation. Here is how it works:

Action!

After you have practiced using these social influence skills for a period of time, and have repeatedly tried a number of different skills, you are ready to evaluate your efforts. First, make two lists. In one of them, put the skills you found to be successful. In the other, list those skills that were consistently unsuccessful. Now, take a plain sheet of paper and divide it vertically into right and left halves, as you did in your "plan ahead" action project. At the top of one of these columns, write "Successful," and at the top of the other, "Unsuccessful."

Look for characteristic differences between the two lists. Read over the list of successful skills. Do you see any common elements running through them? Do they seem to come predominantly from the same category of skills? How would you describe them as a group? Write these things down in the "Successful" column of your divided sheet. Now take a similar look at the "Unsuccessful" list. Do you find the opposite of the characteristics of the successful skills, or are they about the same? Write down everything you see about them in the "Unsuccessful" column. What do these comparative differences and similarities tell you about your choice of skills for exerting social influence?

You can use this same technique for analyzing many aspects of your efforts. For example, by using lists of the *situations* in which you were successful and unsuccessful, you will obtain some clues as to your chances of success with a given type of social pressure.

2. *The "action-outcome" technique.* Here is a way of profiting from your failures.

Action!

First, take a sheet of paper and draw two lines across it, dividing it horizontally into thirds. Now, think back to a recent unsuccessful attempt to carry social influence. Write down across the top of the first third of the paper the action you actually took in this situation. Directly under the action (still in the same box), write what happened (the outcome). Now, across the top of each of the other boxes write down other possible actions *you might have taken* in this situation. (It might take several sheets to list all you can think of.) Under each of these possible actions you are now going to write three things: (1) the *worst possible* outcome that might have resulted from taking this action; (2) the *best* possible outcome that might have resulted; (3) the *most probable* outcome. After studying these possible actions and outcomes, which action do you think you should take if you should meet that same situation again? Which skills will be the most helpful in bringing about the desirable outcome?

3. *Look for evidence from both sides.* A scientist always considers at least two hypotheses when he looks for evidence. One is that his theory is correct, the other that it is incorrect. And most good scientists are more interested in finding evidence to prove themselves *wrong* than evidence to prove themselves right. If they

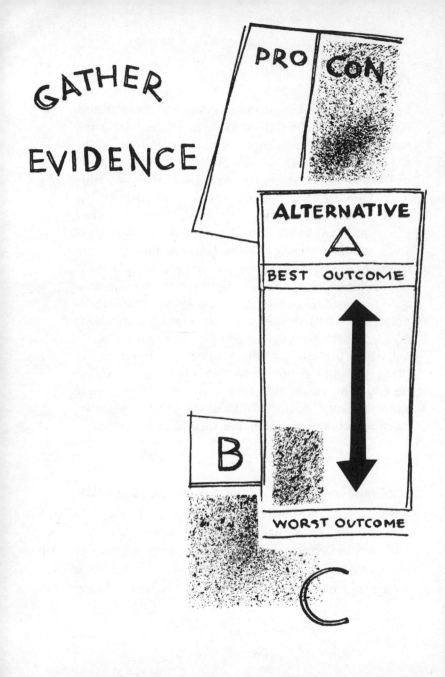

fail to find such evidence, they may then conclude that they were right! You must apply the same criteria in evaluating your efforts to carry social influence. Do not "stack the deck" so that it will come out in your favor. This would be like the child who changes the rules of the game as he goes along in order to win!

4. *Keep things in proper perspective*. Many of the less successful experiences in social influence come about because of fear, particularly fear of failure and fear of criticism. Often, the danger feared is built up out of all proportion to its importance. In evaluating your failures, ask yourself if part of the reason you failed was because of fear that came about when things got out of perspective. Because most of us tend to evaluate the present moment out of all proportion to its importance, it is a good idea to "sleep on it" before making any final decisions about important matters. You will be surprised how much better things look from the perspective of tomorrow morning.

The boy who related the following incident decided on the kind of girl he was looking for, and was not afraid to face the comments and criticisms of those who held different opinions:

I know (the) looks of a girl mean a lot to a boy who is dating her. I am going with a girl now who is not too cute, but in my estimation she has charm, personality, character, morals, etc., which I accept alone as good for a girl. Well, anyway, many boys were accusing me of going with a "scud" and saying that I had had to reach down in the nether part of the earth for her. But, I stood up to what I actually thought of the girl and I was not gullible enough to listen to these false rumors. I would accept a girl for *what* she is, not exactly her looks. You would be surprised how a girl like this is so much more emotionally mature than others.

CHAPTER FOUR

A
Master
Plan

A Master Plan

There you have them—the skills which, if properly used, can help you stand up for your beliefs and make the maximum use of your potential personal power for good. As is true of any great power, however, and especially of the skills of personal relationships, the one crucial question remaining is: "Will I use my personal power for good or evil; for the benefit of others or only for the selfish satisfaction of my own desires?" The dictator, the criminal, the corrupt labor boss or management executive, all use their "skills" to the detriment of society. On the other hand, Joan of Arc, Patrick Henry, Edmund G. Ross and Susan B. Anthony stand among a multitude who applied their abilities to a part of the world's evil and fought, not for personal gain, but for the benefit of all mankind.

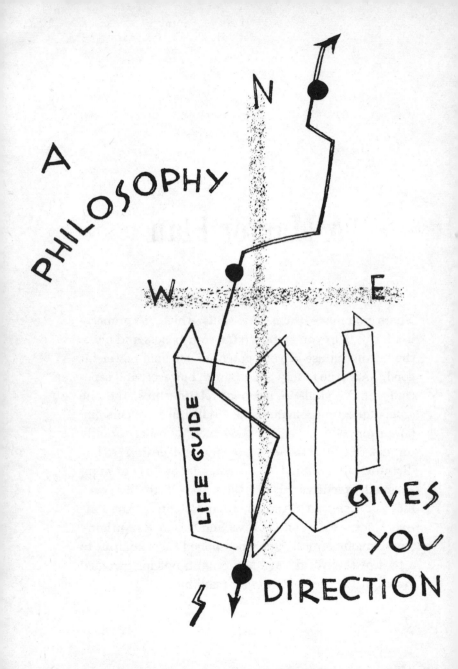

The possession of great power carries with it great responsibilities. The President of the United States, with an awesome arsenal of destruction at his command, lives with the daily responsibility for the life or death of a large part of the world's population! In order to use that power properly, he and his advisers draw up master plans.

The power your fellow teen-agers have placed in your hands through this book must also be used wisely. You, too, should have a master plan to guide your life and determine the use you make of your developing skills of personal power.

Your Philosophy of Life

What we are talking about is your basic philosophy of life. What is that? It is really a combination of many things. It is the result of your thinking about "the big questions" of life: why you were born, who you are, and what you plan to do about it now that you are here. It is the sum total of your attitudes toward life, of all the experiences you have had, all the people you have known. It is hopes and dreams. And it is faith—the kind of faith that restores your sense of direction when you become discouraged or confused.

The most important thing the hundreds of teen-agers who actually "wrote" this book had to say about a philosophy of life—a master plan—is that *it must be your own*. You are a unique individual. There is not another creature in the whole world just like you. Because this is so, you cannot "wear" someone else's philosophy of life like you might wear his overcoat. Your thoughts and dreams are the most private property you possess. Therefore, your philosophy of life, since it represents all your thoughts and attitudes about life rolled into one "package," is your own private property, too. You must roll up your own philosophy of life! But because you are constantly having new experiences and new thoughts, you will never quite get it all rolled up. There is a "growing edge" to your master plan, which should continue to grow for the rest of your life.

It's Time to Decide

That brings us down to the present moment. And in this moment you must make some decisions. You cannot avoid them. Life itself is basically just a long series of decisions. What we often forget is that when we make a decision to do one thing, we are at the same time automatically deciding *not* to do many other things we might have done with that same amount of time. And even if you should decide *not* to decide, you have in that moment made a decision!

What is it that you have to decide right now? Well, at the beginning of this book you made a decision to invest the time to read it (and hopefully to work out the action projects along the way). Now that you have read it, you must decide what you are going to do about it. You must decide who and what you are in relation to what you have read.

The alternatives appear to be clear enough. Either you have some convictions and want to stand for them, or you do not. Either you want to be a more effective person in your relationships with others, or you do not. Your self-respect and personal integrity are either important to you, or they are not. You either have the backbone to *do* something to help yourself stand for what you believe, or you do not. If you have the backbone, you are either willing to give the skills of personal power provided in this book a try, or you are not. In any case, the one thing you cannot avoid at this moment is the making of decisions about these alternatives.

CAUTION! Before you make any "final" decisions, you should be aware of the possible consequences of deciding who and what you are. Such decisions have a way of taking hold of a person, of shaping his destiny into patterns sometimes totally unexpected, or perhaps even "unwanted." For example, there was a young man many centuries ago, a carpenter by trade, who faced many of these crossroads in his life. He, too, had to decide who he was, whether or not he was going to stand up for his beliefs, and just how far he was willing to go to back them up. His decisions ultimately cost him his life. History records that they also led to such an upheaval in human events that this one man's influence is still shaping world events two thousand years later! Such is the power of personal conviction.

But now . . . THE DECISIONS ARE YOURS!